GW00891453

The Marriage Foundation

– By McPeters Atsagbede –

An environmentally friendly book printed and bound in
England by www.printondemand-worldwide.com

Mixed Sources
Product group from well-managed
forests, and other controlled sources
www.fsc.org Cert no. TT-COC-002641
© 1996 Forest Stewardship Council

PEFC Certified
This product is
from sustainably
managed forests
and controlled
sources
www.pefc.org

This book is made entirely of chain-of-custody materials

www.fast-print.net/store.php

THE MARRIAGE FOUNDATION
Copyright © McPeters Atsagbede 2014
E-mail: matsagbede@gmail.com

A catalogue record for this book is
available from the British Library

All Scriptures, unless otherwise stated, are taken from The New King James Version of the Bible, Copyright 1990, Thomas Nelson Inc.

ISBN 978-1-178456-031-7

First published 2014 by
FASTPRINT PUBLISHING
Peterborough, England.

This book is dedicated to all marriages that are built on the foundation of Christ and those that would be built or rebuilt on the foundation of Christ; especially through the reading of this book.

Table of Contents

The Marriage Foundation

Acknowledgements

I am eternally grateful to God for giving me the inspiration to write this book and for His grace that has seen this work through.

For devoting time to meticulously proofread and edit the manuscript, my special appreciation goes to Jeanne Marie Leach. Your comments about the book have been a source of encouragement.

I cannot fully express my sincere appreciation to Pastor Dupe (Dupsy) and Pastor (Mrs) Jackie Omotosho for the invaluable roles they have played in my spiritual life. God used both of you to guide me in the way of my Spiritual Calling and stir up my gifting in Ministry. You have always been a source of support and inspiration. Pastor Dupsy, thank you, once again, for writing the "Foreword" to this book.

To Pastor John and Pastor (Mrs) Stella Toritsemotse I also say a special thank you for all your prayers, support and encouragement. You have aided my spiritual growth tremendously by continually providing me with opportunities to develop in knowledge. Your sincere love and warmth towards the brethren would always be remembered.

To all the Pastors and those from whom I have received spiritual nourishment over the years, I express my gratitude. May you all be constantly refreshed by the Holy Spirit, in Jesus' Name.

I also acknowledge my spiritual family, The Redeemed Christian Church of God, Fountain of Love, Naas; as well as The Redeemed Christian Church of God, Open Heavens, Glasnevin. Your prayers, love and support are much appreciated.

Finally, my profound appreciation goes to my wife, Sandra and our children, Daisy, Dennie and Deborah. I thank you especially for your love, understanding and support all through the years. In you I have found a mirror to constantly reflect, evaluate and bring myself under God's divine pruning, so as to be the husband and father that God expects me to be.

Foreword

I enjoyed the privilege of being pastor to McPeters and his lovely wife Sandra for some years. The love, joy and peace in their marriage and their home were evident to all. These and their wonderful hospitality made their home the most successful house fellowship in the church. The success of their marriage qualifies McPeters to write this book.

Uncle McPee, as we fondly call him, is a man of great wisdom and revelation! His explanation on roles and responsibilities in marriage is so revealing. He offers biblical answers and guidance to the usual questions on marriage in our society. He also gives a good argument on why we need to do away with the terms "Breadwinner" and "Housewife".

The book - The Marriage Foundation - takes us back to the one who created marriage, to establish a biblical foundation for marriage.

This book is a compelling read for wisdom, revelation and counsel for those about to marry and those who are already married. It invites us to make God an integral part of our marriage. It also helps us to understand the purpose, roles and responsibilities inherent in marriage, while encouraging us to live up to God's expectation of us in the marriage.

Pastor Dupe Omotosho
RCCG Jesus City Church
1218 Copeland Oaks Drive
Morrisville NC 27560

Introduction

The Family is considered the basic unit of society. But much more than being the basic unit, it is the bedrock of society. Therefore, it is not presumptuous to say that there can be no meaningful discussion about family and society without some mention of marriage.

Marriage is a subject that has always generated a lot of interest in society—both to those who believe in it and those who claim not to believe in it. This is understandable, considering the role marriage plays in the family and society.

In this book I have chosen to look at marriage critically from its very root or foundation. Where the foundation of a building is faulty, there is every tendency that whatever structure is put on that foundation will collapse. So, also, it is with marriage. This is why the Scripture says in Psalm 11:3 that "If the foundations are destroyed what can the righteous do?" The only viable and reasonable thing to do is to return to that foundation and seek to rebuild or correct it.

While quite a list of literature, seminars, and counselling abound on this subject, few are focused on the foundational truth about marriage. It is made worse in today's world where we try to be socially and politically correct in what we say. Attempts also are being made to subject the Word of God to this social and political correctness. The truth, however, is that God's Word is forever sure and bears the same truth whether in Africa, America, Asia, or Europe. It is also as true today as it was yesterday. So any "truth" that changes with time, persons, environment, and culture cannot be God's truth and should be subject to proper scrutiny.

A lot of attention and time is being focused and spent on the things that "spice up" a marriage instead of on the things that are the solid foundation on which every marriage must rest. Some of these marriage "spices" have socio-cultural and ethnic relativity while the things that are foundational hold true universally. Sometimes, those spices have only become needed because we want to make up for certain deficiencies in our "marriage cooking." Just like in normal cooking, the spices may not have been necessary if the "marriage cooking" was right in the first place.

Marriage was never meant to be burdensome and should never be viewed as such. Instead, God meant it to be a burden lifter. The fact that some people now think and see marriage as a burden is not new. After Jesus explained God's original plan for marriage in Matthew 19:1-10, it is recorded that His disciples said: "If such is the case of the man with his wife, it is better not to marry." Apostle Paul also took this line of thought when he said, "For I wish that all men were even as I myself" (1 Corinthians 7: 7). He then went ahead to advise those not yet married to remain unmarried just like him. This shows that some of the Apostles also viewed marriage as burdensome.

If God had said in His Word that it is not good for a man to be alone but should have a wife for a companion, and man now says otherwise, whose report should we believe? Certainly that of God! Jesus is our sure foundation. There is no other foundation that can be laid by anyone except that which had been laid by Jesus (1 Corinthians 3: 11). No other foundation can sustain marriage except the Word of God. Those disciples declared being unmarried as better than being married. This is because they were looking at marriage principally from two angles: something to satisfy sexual desires (and possibly raise offspring), and something that should be easily dissolved at will. They were, therefore, uncomfortable with Jesus' exposition. But the purpose of marriage goes far beyond that.

Being married or unmarried is not necessarily the criteria for being a good Christian or making it to heaven. But what you do with your marriage can have

consequences that could affect you before
God. For example:

- Did you become a liar in the course of
  your marriage by lying to your spouse?
- Did you become abusive in your
  relationship with your spouse?
- Did you become unfaithful and unreliable
  due to your infidelity to your spouse?
- Did you become a wicked person through
  acting wickedly to your spouse?
- Did you act to support and encourage or
  to pull and discourage your spouse away
  from God?
- Did you act responsibly in raising the
  children that God entrusted to you
  through marriage?

Remember that we are all accountable to a
God who knows and sees all things. Some
typical examples of how our actions in
marriage can affect us before God are: Onan
and Tamar (Genesis 38: 6-10) and David and
Michal (2 Samuel 6: 16-23).

Until Onan married Tamar, following the
tradition of his people, he was safe. But once
married to Tamar, he became answerable to
God for his actions towards his wife, Tamar.
Hence he was struck dead for dealing with
Tamar treacherously by deliberately emitting
on the ground each time during love making.

In Michal's case, for despising and
dishonouring David, her husband, God closed

her womb and caused her to be barren until death.

It is in this light that we need to carefully understand what God expects of us in marriage and how we can indeed enjoy and have a glorious marriage that meets the expectation of God.

The Marriage Foundation

– By McPeters Atsagbede –

The Marriage Foundation

Definition

The way we define a thing or situation determines how we relate to it and ultimately, the outcome we get or experience. It is often said that as you make your bed, so you lie on it.

This holds very true for marriage relationships. The way you define marriage would determine how you relate in and to your marriage. Ultimately, it would determine what you get *in your marriage* and *out of your marriage.* So the issue of definition is as important as the marriage itself.

In today's society, marriage is being defined and redefined, depending upon whose interest is involved. But if we stop for a moment to ponder on this attempt at redefining marriage, we would realise that it is as wanting to redefine who a man or a woman is.

Marriage is an institution that is as old as mankind. It was designed and ordained by God. It is, therefore, only in the original plan of the designer—God—that we can experience the full potentials and benefits of marriage.

In today's world, we tend to think that marriage is a social contract between two individuals, normally between a man and a woman. Even where it is considered as a covenant due to better understanding, it is still generally considered to be a covenant between only the two parties.

This is one of the greatest errors of marriage that has been the bane of wrecked, dysfunctional, and traumatized marriages.

Marriage, in the definition of God, is a covenant between two parties—a man and a woman—with God as the anchor or bond.

In any marriage that is ordained by God, He is always present as an essential party.

"And they heard the sound of the Lord God walking in the garden in the cool of the day, and Adam and his wife hid themselves from the presence of the Lord God among the trees of the garden" (Genesis 3:8-11).

Also, when King Abimelech took Abraham's wife, Sarah, even though ignorantly, God was there to ensure restoration and prevent defilement.

"Now Abraham said of Sarah his wife, 'She is my sister.' And Abimlech King of Grar sent and took Sarah. But God came to Abimelech in a dream by night, and said to him, 'Indeed you are a dead man because of the woman whom you have taken, for she is a man's wife'" (Genesis 20:2-3).

Joseph realised this; hence, he told Potipher's wife that he could not sleep with her and sin against God. Even though they were Egyptians, Joseph being a Jew had been brought up to know that God is part of a marriage covenant.

"And it came to pass after these things that his master's wife cast longing eyes on Joseph, and she said, 'Lie with me,' but he refused and said to his master's wife, 'Look, my master does not know what is with me in the house, and he has committed all that he has to my hand. There is no one greater in this house than I, nor has he kept back anything from me but you, because you are his wife. How then can I do this great wickedness, *and sin against God*?'" (Genesis 39:7-9 Italics are by author for emphasis).

Another point to prove the fact that God is present and is indeed part of every marriage ordained by Him is the account of Adam and Eve.

The Scripture records that Adam and Eve were both naked and were not ashamed until they sinned.

Now, who were they not ashamed of? Certainly, it could not have been of themselves. The shame was referring to their nakedness in the presence of God who was always around them. Recall that after they sinned, they were still together in their nakedness but now unable to stand before the presence of God.

"And they were both naked, the man and his wife, and were not ashamed" (Genesis 2:25). "And they heard the sound of the Lord God walking in the garden in the cool of the day, and Adam and his wife hid themselves from the presence of the Lord God among the trees of the garden. Then the Lord God called to Adam and said to him, 'Where are you?' So he said, 'I heard Your voice in the garden, and I was afraid because I was naked; and I hid myself'" (Genesis 3:8-10).

A final point to show that God is part of every marriage ordained by Him can be learned from the account of Onan and Tamar.

"And Judah said to Onan, 'Go in to your brother's wife and marry her, and raise up an heir to your brother.' But Onan knew that the heir would not be his; and it came to pass, when he went in to his brother's wife, that he emitted on the ground, lest he should give an heir to his brother. And the thing which he did displeased the Lord; therefore He killed him also" (Genesis 38:8-10).

From this account it becomes evident that even in love making between a husband and the wife, the Lord is present. This is why married couples should be afraid of breaking their marriage vows by engaging in extra-marital affairs. They should understand that as the anchor of that marriage vow they took,

God's presence is always with them to uphold and defend the marriage. By engaging in that extra-marital affair, which negates the marriage vow, the guilty party might just be courting God's wrath upon himself or herself.

God is always present and is an integral part of every marriage ordained by Him.

This is what has been corrupted in certain cultures. In an attempt to replicate this marriage order, they involve their local deities during marriage rites by making such deities the anchor of the marriage covenant. The deities are then expected to protect, defend, and give out punishment against acts that are contrary to the marriage covenants, such as infidelity and gross wickedness.

God's original definition of marriage can be established from the first union that He brought into being—Adam and Eve. It was between one man and one woman, not one man and two or more women, man and man, or woman and woman.

Today, people are constantly trying to define and redefine marriage and have entered into marriage relationships based on such definitions. As Christians, however, who should know that it is always better to go by the perfect will of God, our definition must align with God's original design and definition of marriage. Doing otherwise would be working against God's will or only in His permissive will, which always has consequences.

Polygamy, some may argue, is not new and has been there with the Israelites and was even practised by notable men like David. It was also there in the early church, hence the recommendation in the book of Timothy 3 that in appointing Church leaders, consideration should be given only to those with one wife. Polygamy, however, has its root in covetousness, greed, envy, wickedness, and rebellion. The first recorded case of a man with two wives was that of Lamech, a descendant of Cain, the murderer.

"And Cain knew his wife, and she conceived and bore Enoch . . . To Enoch was born Irad; and Irad begot Mehujael, and Mehujael begot Methushael, and Methushael begot Lamech. Then Lamech took for himself two wives: the name of one was Adah, and the name of the second was Zillah" (Genesis 4:17-19).

Lamech was a murderer also, as he later confessed to his wives:

"Then Lamech said to his wives, 'Adah and Zillah, hear my voice; wives of Lamech, listen to my speech! For I have killed a man for wounding me, even a young man for hurting me. If Cain shall be avenged sevenfold, then Lamech seventy-sevenfold'" (Genesis 4:23-24)

Now, with the origin of polygamy exposed, would this be a role model that any descent and God fearing man would want to emulate? I would not think so. It is very clear for anyone to see how the seed of covetousness sown by Cain came to bear its fruit in his descendant, Lamech.

No wonder men who marry more than one wife are men who are covetous and never satisfied with what they already have.

Key Point

The world, especially today, is saying that marriage is a social contract freely entered into by two individuals, irrespective of who they are.

It is also saying that even though united in marriage, the partners are still two separate individuals with each having his or her inalienable rights of freedom.

But God is saying to us as Christians, that marriage is a sacred covenant between two individuals, a man and a woman with God as the centre piece.

God is also saying to us as Christians, that the sacred covenant of marriage unites the two as one in Him, through Jesus Christ. So we are no longer two separate individuals with each having his or her inalienable rights of freedom but now one, united in God through

Jesus Christ, in thought, words, deeds, purpose, pursuits and in spirit.

Purpose of Marriage

Another very important factor of marriage is the purpose. Why do you want to get married?

Quite a number of people have experienced disappointments in their marriages because they entered into it for the wrong reason. Some have entered into marriage, which is meant to be a lifelong relationship, in order to satisfy a short term purpose.

Are you getting married in order to end family and societal pressures emanating from being single?

Are you getting married so as to have someone who would share your financial burden?

Are you getting married as a way of ending your long battle with sexual lust?

Are you getting married so you can now be considered "responsible" by society?

Are you getting married because you want to have children that are not outside of marriage?

Are you getting married because you have found someone so beautiful or handsome that you do not want to lose her or him?

Are you getting married because it is in God's plan for you, and you are being led by the Spirit of God to marry?

As weird as some of the questions above may sound, the reality is that they are sometimes, if not most times, the driver of our actions concerning marriage. When marriage is entered into for the wrong purpose, even where the intention appears good, it will most likely end up with disappointments, frustrations, and struggles.

For instance, if you marry because of family or societal pressures, what happens when you now begin to experience other pressures from those angles after the marriage?

Similarly, if you marry principally because you need someone to share your financial burden, what happens if your spouse becomes unable to support you financially?

Also, if you marry because of beauty or natural endowment, what happens if the beauty or endowment is no longer there?

Equally, if you marry in order to satisfy your sexual lust, what happens if your spouse is no longer able to satisfy your sexual desires?

The Scripture tells us that in the beginning, before God institutionalized marriage, he advanced a purpose for the man to have a wife. "And the Lord God said, 'It is not good that man should be alone; I will make him a helper comparable to him.' But for Adam there was not found a helper comparable to him" (Genesis 2:18-20).

Before going into marriage you need to seek and know God's purpose for you so that marriage should aid you in that purpose and not hinder you. God made the man and his wife to be helpers of each other's divine purpose because our God himself is a helper. "Behold, God is my Helper; The Lord is with those who uphold my life" (Psalm 54:4).

Remember that God created us in His own image and "likeness". If God is a helper and created us in His image and likeness, then we must by that nature be helpers of one another in fulfilling our God-given destiny and purpose. Therefore, our purpose of marriage should be to have a companion either as a husband or a wife who can help us to fulfil our divine purpose in life, just as we also help them (our spouses) to fulfil their divine purpose with the divine help of God; working through the Holy Spirit who has been given to us as our Helper.

The Scripture records that the combination of husband and wife working in unity with God through the help of the Holy Spirit is able to accomplish much more than working individually. Hence, we are told that while one can chase off a thousand, the combination of the husband and the wife working together as a team can chase off ten thousand, with the help of God.

We are also told that a three-piece cord cannot be broken easily. "Though one may be overpowered by another, two can withstand him. And a threefold cord is not quickly broken" (Ecclesiastics 4:12).

So marriage is part of God's plan for helping us to fulfil our purpose in life and must not be taken or treated as something independent of our divine purpose.

The Choice of a Partner

This is one area where we have been most challenged. Early after creation, man was given the freedom of choice by God. This seemingly simple but complex phenomenon has been the bane of mankind. Even in our society today, this concept of "freedom" has continued to pose challenges in its form and expressions that are better imagined than seen or experienced.

Even though God gave man the freedom of choice, man was never left unguided by Him. God would always make His own will known in the matter but would leave the ultimate choice of decision to us. As a guide, He would sometimes, if not most times, even tell us of the consequences of the decisions we make based on the alternative choices presented to us. It is, however, tragic that in spite of God's guidance, man has continued to make wrong choices that have always brought us devastating consequences.

Early after creation, in the Garden of Eden, God told man about all the trees, fruits, and vegetables available to man as food. He also told man those that were good as food and the one that was not good as food and the consequences of eating it. Yet in making his choice, man ignored God's guiding counsel and ate the forbidden fruit.

"And the Lord God commanded the man saying, 'Of every tree of the garden you may freely eat; but of the tree of the knowledge of good and evil you shall not eat, for in the day that you eat of it you shall surely die'" (Genesis 2:16-17).

Likewise, after God gave the Israelites the Ten Commandments through Moses, He told them of the consequences of obeying the commandments and that of disobeying them. He then left them with the choices.

"See, I have set before you today life and good, death and evil, in that I command you today to love the Lord your God, to walk in His Ways, and to keep His commandments, His statutes, and His judgements, that you may live and multiply; and the Lord your God will bless you in the land which you go to possess. But if your heart turns away so that you do not hear, and are drawn away, and worship other gods and serve them, I announce to you today that you shall surely perish; you shall not prolong your days in the land which you cross over the Jordan to go in and possess. I call heaven and earth as witnesses today against you, that I have set before you life and death, blessing and cursing; therefore choose life, that both you and your descendants may live" (Deuteronomy 30:15-19).

God always guides us to enable us make the right choices, but the ultimate decision as to the choice is ours to make.

As relates to marriage, God has prepared a partner for everyone who is being led by Him into marriage, just as He prepared Eve for Adam. We must, however, have to ask for His guidance to choose the right partner that He has prepared for us—especially now (unlike in the time of Adam) that we may have a number of other "contestants" presenting themselves as alternative choices. We should also crave for a discerning spirit so that we can recognise our God-given partner when we see them; otherwise we could miss them and settle for the wrong choice.

Adam recognised Eve as his wife without God saying so. The moment God woke him up and brought the woman before him, he declared her as his wife. He did not have to ask God who the woman was, what he needed to do with her, or if there were others that God has also made for him.

"And Adam said: 'This is now bone of my bones and flesh of my flesh; she shall be called Woman, because she was taken out of Man'" (Genesis 2:23).

We also see that when Isaac was led to marry, both the father, Abraham, and the servant who was sent on the mission sought God's guidance in the choice of a wife for Isaac. Hence, it is no surprise that the servant recognised Isaac's wife the moment he saw her. Isaac also recognised and acknowledged the wife the moment he saw her.

However, when we compare this to the situation with his son, Jacob, things are somehow different.

Jacob fled home for his safety, having cheated his brother, Esau, regarding his birthright. His purpose for going to his Uncle Laban was not originally to seek a wife; hence, he did not ask God at any time for guidance about choosing a wife. Having been captivated by her physical beauty, he acted on the basis of his emotions to ask Laban for Rachel as his wife. On the other hand, Rachel's sister, Leah, who Jacob never really fancied much, was being prepared for him by God acting through Laban. Despite all the spiteful treatment meted out to Leah, God was favourably disposed to her in the marriage and was even fighting on her behalf. It is recorded that God closed Rachel's womb while blessing Leah with children because God saw that Leah was not loved. It took the intercession of Jacob (whom God loved) to open the womb of Rachel again.

Of the twelve sons of Jacob, who became the founding fathers of the twelve tribes of Israel, Leah had six, with most of the notable children coming out of her.

- She was the mother of Issachar, whose sons were noted for their exceptional gifting in the interpretation of signs
- She was also the mother of Levi, who became blessed with the priesthood
- Judah, through whose lineage our Lord Jesus was born, came from Leah

Rachel almost brought destruction to the family of Jacob when she stole the father's god and took it with her on their journey back to Canaan. This shows she was not fully committed to the God of Jacob, despite knowing that God was with him.

It took the death of Rachel for Jacob's eyes to become opened to the fact that Leah was his God-ordained wife. Hence, he buried Leah in their ancestral land and requested to be buried alongside Leah at his death. Rachel was not given a similar honour at her burial.

So while we have the freedom to choose our partners, we must do this through God's guidance in order to ensure that our choice is indeed God's choice for us. Any wrong choice made in marriage has dire consequences which we may be forced to live with for the rest of our lives—either within the marriage or outside of the marriage.

Key Point

If God is in that marriage plan, He will guide you in the way of the right choice if you seek his guidance, but the ultimate decision of choosing the partner is yours to make.

The ability to choose is an indication of true freedom while the ability to deal with the consequences of choice is the price of freedom.

Prayerfully ask therefore for a discerning spirit so you do not get confused or carried away by those who are competing and presenting themselves as alternative choices.

The Roles and Responsibilities of Partners

When we talk about the role of partners, what readily comes to mind is the distribution of the chores:

- Who does the laundry?
- Who does the dishes?
- Who does the cooking?
- Who does the baby-sitting?
- Who pays what bills?
- Who does the school runs and other errands?

Sometimes there is a lot of rancour in the home over whose duty it is to carry out these tasks. Unnecessary and avoidable friction has been created in homes because the partners have chosen to focus on these, using worldly standards as yardsticks, before even thinking of what their God-given role is in their marriage relationship. Whenever we do this, we drain the substance out of the subject and reduce it to a mere shadow of its essence. No doubt it is necessary for someone to administer these tasks for the home to run smoothly. However, understanding our God-given roles make it easier for us to take them on and perform excellently.

In today's world where there is so much talk about "gender equality," "affirmative action," "human rights," and "freedom," it is very easy to offend the sensibilities of a number of people in looking at this subject, even where it is not intended. But a conscious attempt would be made to explore and examine the issue here, in the light of God's Word that is ever true.

While environment, situations, and circumstances may define the roles couple play in a marriage relationship, such definitions may not hold true for all occasions. However, if dictated by the Word of God, the roles would hold true always, no matter the environment, situation, or circumstance.

Most of the friction generated by the issue of each partner's role in a marriage relationship stem from the fact that people tend to misconstrue the term *role* for *responsibility*. These are two different things and must not be confused for one another.

Roles are complimentary in nature, and therefore come together to form or produce a unified whole. Being complimentary, they are neither competing nor conflicting. They could be diffused such that anyone can take on a particular role.

Responsibilities, on the other hand, do not necessarily have to be complimentary. The focus is more on ownership and accountability.

Roles

The role of partners in a marriage relationship is to complement one another, with the common goal of producing a marriage where there is harmony, lasting love, friendship, and above all, working in the unity of God's purpose. In this regard, partners must never see themselves as competing with one another and must never take on roles that are at cross-purpose with their common goal in marriage.

In practical terms, it means that even when as partners we agree that a particular task is the responsibility of the man or the woman, the other partner should readily step in to take on that role if the need arises. Also, in taking on that role he or she must not see it as a failure on the part of the other partner but a complimentary effort to ensure that their common goal is achieved. The partner stepping in to take the role of the other as a helper must do it to the best of his or her abilities, even though not responsible for that particular role. This is because even where we are not responsible, we are still answerable to God for each of our actions.

For us to be very effective in our marriage roles, God would normally give us certain special gifts or endowments that would make us best suited for those roles. We would, therefore, observe that we normally excel in those roles with minimal effort and stress or still find joy in doing it despite the stress.

Let us take a look at certain people who played complimentary roles as husband and wife.

Abraham and Sarah took on complimentary roles in the entertainment of the guest angels. Even though it was Abraham that arranged the hosting, the Scriptures record that both Abraham and Sarah were involved in the preparation and presentation of the food to their guest.

"Then the Lord appeared to him by the terebinth trees of Mamre, as he was sitting in the tent door in the heat of the day. So he lifted his eyes and looked, and behold, three men were standing by him; and when he saw them, he ran from the tent door to meet them, and bowed himself to the ground, and said, 'My Lord, if I have now found favour in your sight, do not pass on by Your servant. Please let a little water be brought, and wash your feet, and rest yourselves under the tree. And I will bring a morsel of bread, that you may refresh your hearts. After that you may pass by, inasmuch as you have come to your servant.'

"They said, 'Do as you have said.' So Abraham hurried into the tent to Sarah and said, 'Quickly, make ready three measures of fine meal; knead it and make cakes."

And Abraham ran to the herd, took a tender and good calf, gave it to a young man, and he hastened to prepare it. So he took butter and milk and the calf which he had prepared, and set it before them; and he stood by them under the tree as they ate" (Genesis 18:1-7).

We can see that in the preparation of the meal, while Sarah was making the cakes, Abraham was busy with the calf. He was also involved in the presentation and played the role of the waiter.

Another example is Nabal and Abigail as told in 1Samuel 25:2-38

Here we see that even though Nabal has responsibility for his family, he had jeopardized their lives with his foolish and thoughtless act of selfishness toward David. Abigail did not play the blaming game nor did she insist that her husband must play his rightful role in fixing the problem he had created. Instead, sensing that a delay could be dangerous, she stepped in and took the necessary corrective action to save the situation. Even David acknowledged that fact in his statement to her.

"Then David said to Abigail, 'Blessed is the Lord God of Israel, who sent you this day to meet me! And blessed is your advice and blessed are you, because you have kept me this day from coming to bloodshed and from avenging myself with my own hand. For indeed, as the Lord God of Israel lives, who has kept me back from hurting you, unless you had hurried and come to meet me, surely by morning light no males would have been left to Nabal!'

"So David received from her hand what she had brought him, and said to her, 'Go up in peace to your house. See, I have heeded your voice and respected your person'" (I Samuel 25:32-35).

Responsibilities

Responsibilities have to do with ownership and accountability. It means being in charge and answerable for the actions and inactions, conduct, activities, and performances of person(s) or thing(s) that one is in control of. It also means knowing that one is in charge and not assuming that others would take ownership.

As a result of the burden that comes with responsibilities, which could be huge, it is often necessary to define and agree on who is in charge. This is why we find situations where people are made to answer for the action of others who, by the definition, are not answerable for their own actions.

For example, a little child or even an adult who is considered to be of unsound mind would normally not be answerable or responsible for their actions, no matter how grievous. Instead, someone else who ought to have been in charge would be held accountable.

So also it is and should be for marriage. For a marriage relationship to work well, the partners should define and agree on their areas of responsibilities, both individually and jointly. This is not for the purpose of fault-finding but to help the partners reinforce their sense of duty.

Where they need the help of others (including their partners) to achieve the goal, they should ask and not assume that those other people ought to know.

Also, after enlisting the support of their partners or others, they should still follow through to ensure that the particular task is completely executed, knowing that they are ultimately still responsible for the final outcome.

Needless arguments and tension have sometimes arisen in homes because the partners were each assuming that the other ought to have known and acted accordingly.

For instance, let us take a situation where it has been agreed between the husband and the wife that the wife is responsible for dinner at home.

If for any particular reason she is unable to perform the task, she should not just assume that the husband would understand or step in to do it for her. Even where she knows he would do it, she should still lovingly approach him and ask for his help with the dinner.

There could be homes where there is a maid or grown-up children or relatives that can do the dinner. Yet, taking responsibility demands that the wife should still follow through with whoever is engaged to do the dinner to ensure that the right meal is prepared and served at the appropriate time.

Never assume or take your partner for granted over your responsibilities.

Another example could be where it has been agreed between the husband and the wife that the husband is responsible for the house rent.

He should not assume that because he has lost his job, the wife would understand that the responsibility of paying the rent has automatically transferred to her. Even where she is in a position to pay and is willing to pay, the man should lovingly ask for support from his wife.

Taking responsibility means knowing and acknowledging that though the wife is helping with the rent, the responsibility for ensuring that the rent is paid is still his.

In the beginning, God made man the spiritual head of the family. This means that the man is meant to be the priest of the family and is accountable to God for those under his leadership.

As priest of the family, the man is to draw down the presence of God and cause the family to focus on God and experience His divine presence in their lives. The wife is to be a pillar of support as a joint priest with the man to ensure that the man does not fail in this calling.

Spiritually, the responsibility for his family is primarily that of the husband even though the wife is there to encourage and support him. The man is supposed to be the visionary in the home, ensuring that the family is guided and led according to God's expectation.

One of the reasons God revealed to Abraham what he was going to do to Sodom and Gomorrah was because He knew Abraham had responsibility for leading his household in the way of God.

"And the Lord said, 'Shall I hide from Abraham what I am doing? Since Abraham shall surely become a great and mighty nation, and all the nations of the earth shall be blessed in him. For I have known him, in order that he may command his children and his household after him, that they keep the way of the Lord, to do righteousness and justice, that the Lord may bring to Abraham what He has spoken to him" (Genesis 18:17-19).

We can see from the Scriptures that Abraham was expected to take responsibility for leading the way and ensuring that his children and household follow in his steps. Similarly, the man should always bear this consciousness in his everyday affairs in the home.

Also, when Jesus' life was in danger because of Herod, God sent His angel to Joseph and not Mary. Equally, when it was time for them to return with Jesus as a child, the angel was once again sent to Joseph. This shows that God expected Joseph to be responsible for getting his family to safety.

Key points

Roles are meant to be complimentary, so partners should readily take on those ones that would compliment and support each other's effort. However, in doing this, the partner with responsibility for the function must realise that he or she is accountable for the outcome of actions taken and should therefore take charge; even if the assistance of others have to be enlisted for the role.

Leadership, Authority and Submission

Leadership

Leadership is crucial in marriage just as it is in human organisations and society. In very simplistic terms, it presupposes that there is one who gives direction and another or others who follow.

There is a growing class of people who believe and argue that in a marriage relationship there is no leader, as both are equal partners. They believe that ascribing leadership or headship to one of the partners is tantamount to discrimination, which is contrary to God's Word.

Consequently, the attempt here would be to examine leadership in marriage in the light of God's Word.

First, does leadership erode equality?

To answer this, I would want us to take a look at some practical examples and situations.

In a football team, we would normally have players of different talents playing from different angles, each a master of his game. They are all individually talented in their own right. But for the effective coordination of the team, they would pick out a captain from among themselves in conjunction with their Coach and Manager. This does not make the one chosen as the Captain to be more talented than the others, nor the others to be of less importance than the Captain. Rather, it helps to streamline the coordination and management of the team for better and more efficient performance. In recognition of this, the other team mates would normally defer to their Captain and accord him due respect as the Captain of their team.

Similarly, if individuals or friends of equal standing come together to form a business, they would normally have to elect one from among themselves to be the Chairperson of their Board of Directors. This does not make the Chairperson more important than fellow stakeholders or board members—some of whom may have more shares or knowledge than the Chairperson. But again, in recognition of the role, other board members would normally accord due respect to the chosen Chairperson.

The Scriptures recall that even though Jesus is God, He did not consider it an act of inequality or discrimination to become man and die for our sins.

"Let this mind be in you which was also in Christ Jesus, who, being in the form of God, did not consider it robbery to be equal with God, but made Himself of no reputation, taking the form of a bondservant, and coming in the likeness of men. And being found in appearance as a man, He humbled Himself and became obedient to the point of death, even the death of the cross" (Philippians 2:5-8).

It is in this same vein that the Scripture refers to the man as the head of the woman in a marriage relationship, just as Christ is the Head of the Church.

"Wives, submit to your own husbands, as to the Lord. For the husband is head of the wife, as also Christ is head of the church; and He is the Saviour of the body. Therefore, just as the church is subject to Christ, so let the wives be to their own husbands in everything" (Ephesians 5:22-24).

This is the bit that some people now find offensive and consider gender discrimination. But it is the Word of God and cannot be faulted. I would, however, attempt a study of this Scripture here, just to see if it is our understanding or interpretation of the Scripture that is faulty.

What does it mean when I allude to the man as the head of the woman?

All through Scriptures, God has always used the things that we can relate to in getting His message across to us. So here we shall be looking at the anatomy of the body—the head, in particular.

First, let us look at the relationship between the head and other parts of the body.

The Scripture gives us a very vivid account of this.

"For as the body is one and has many members, but all the members of that one body, being many, are one body, so also is Christ. For by one Spirit we were all baptized into one body—whether Jews or Greeks, whether slaves or free—and have all been made to drink into one Spirit. For in fact the body is not one member but many.

"If the foot should say, 'Because I am not a hand, I am not of the body,' is it therefore not of the body?

"And if the ear should say, 'Because I am not an eye, I am not of the body,' is it therefore not of the body?

"If the whole body were an eye, where would be the hearing? If the whole were hearing, where would be the smelling? But now God has set the members, each one of them, in the body just as He pleased. And if they were all one member, where would the body be? But now indeed there are many members, yet one body" (I Corinthians 12:12-20).

From the analysis given in this Scripture, we can see that the head is as important as other parts of the body. They all need each other to function effectively.

So also it is with the man and his wife. Even as head of the family, he needs the support of the wife to be able to function effectively, just as the wife also needs the support of her husband.

Being head does not make the wife to be inferior to the husband; neither does it make the man to be superior to the wife.

Another analogy is that of the coin. We are familiar with the notion that there is a head and there is also a tail of a coin. Yet being a single coin, wherever you find the head that is where the tail would be also. You can never find a coin with the head in one place and the tail in another place.

The above scenarios partly explain why some strongly feel both the man and his wife are equal and, therefore, are opposed to the notion of the man being the head or leader of the marriage union.

If the relationship between the head and the other parts of the body were only as enumerated above, then those opposed to the notion of man being head or leader would have been justified.

However, there are other functions performed by the head that allows it to enjoy the privilege of being honoured as leader of the body.

The head is where the brain is located, into which flows all the nerve systems from the other parts of the body. The nerve-ends at the other parts of the body cannot decipher messages on their own. They have to transmit it to the brain that then decodes and interprets it and transmits it back to that part of the body for necessary action or reaction.

For example, neither the leg nor the hand would sense the danger of being hurt if the brain does not provide them with this information. The leg or hand on its own cannot interpret that fire is dangerous and so can readily move into a flaming fire. All it does is send a signal to the brain as to what is within its surroundings. It is upon receipt of the return signal from the brain telling the leg or hand that the object in question is fire and that it is hot and harmful to come in contact with, that the leg or hand now retreats.

If the brain gives a wrong interpretation, the leg or hand would fall victim to the danger.

So we can see from this illustration that even though all parts of the body are equally important, the other parts concede to the brain (which is part of the head) the role of leadership in guiding the other parts, for the smooth and effective functioning of the overall body.

It is in this vein also that when there is a toss of the coin to decide a game, whoever picks the head is given the honour or privilege of starting the game or making the first choice.

Secondly, let us look at the position of the head on the body.

The head is physically above other parts of the body. In it, we have the eyes, the ears and the mouth—the three key elements needed for a Priest. The head is endowed with vision, hearing, and prophesying.

By grace, God has made man the spiritual head and priest of his family and should be able to lead the family in the vision of God and should be prophesying God's purpose in their lives.

No wonder the Scriptures record that God made all living creatures to pass through Adam, and whatever name Adam called them became their name.

"Out of the ground the Lord God formed every beast of the field and every bird of the air, and brought them to Adam to see what he would call them. And whatever Adam called each living creature, that was its name" (Genesis 2:19)

God also indicated this fact of man being the spiritual head and priest of his family when He had to tell Abraham about His plans to destroy Sodom and Gomorrah.

"And the Lord said, 'Shall I hide from Abraham what I am doing since Abraham shall surely become a great and mighty nation, and all the nations of the earth shall be blessed in him? For I have known him, in order that he may command his children and his household after him, that they keep the way of the Lord, to do righteousness and justice, that the Lord may bring to Abraham what He has spoken to him'" (Genesis 18:17-18).

It should be noted that after Adam and Eve fell as a result of their sin and played the blame game, God reprimanded them with a curse. But interestingly, even in the midst of the curse, God instituted order into the family. God told the woman that from that moment her desire shall be to her husband. This means that unlike the situation where the woman listened to the voice of the serpent without consideration for her husband's opinion, from that moment the woman would cherish her husband's opinion and thoughts on all matters involving them. She would have to submit to her husband.

"To the woman He said, 'I will greatly multiply your sorrow and your conception; in pain you shall bring forth children; your desire shall be for your husband, and he shall rule over you" (Genesis 3:16).

This aspect is actually not a curse but was intended to bring order into the family. Had this order existed in the first place, the woman would likely have waited to seek her husband's opinion before going ahead with the evil counsel of the serpent. This statement is saying that the woman would desire her husband's opinion, interest, and affection above that of others.

Everyone has a leadership capacity and is indeed a leader in one form or the other. There are areas where the wife operates in a leadership capacity, and sometimes there are even areas where the children do the same. For instance, older siblings could take on leadership positions over their younger ones in the home. However, when it comes to the overall leadership of the family, God has entrusted this to the husband and expects him to faithfully perform this role.

Some men have put their wives in difficult situations through a lack of exhibiting leadership, while some wives have taken on for themselves unnecessary antagonism and resentment for actions that portray them as the leaders and for undermining their husbands' leadership position.

For example, it is good for husband and wife to always discuss issues, especially those affecting the family. However, it is equally good that after taking a position (whether it was unanimous or a compromise), the husband should put on his leadership shoes and take responsibility for the action resulting from their decision. There are situations where the wife has been left wounded or portrayed in bad light because the husband had inadvertently exposed her to those who feel offended by their decision, by his not taking on the leadership role.

A typical example might be where someone has requested some assistance from the family. It is alright to respond that you would need to discuss this with your wife or husband first and revert back to the person later. But consider an instance where the husband had responded that he was okay with the request but needed to discuss it with his wife before making a final decision. If after discussing with his wife, he goes to say that he was sorry but the request could not be granted, he would have portrayed the wife as the one who was against the request and may have created unnecessary and avoidable animosity towards her by the one who had made the request. This is simply because he had initially admitted that the request was okay with him before ever discussing it with his wife.

Similarly, a wife who creates the impression that her husband's input is unnecessary, as she is the one who makes the decisions, would have undermined her husband's leadership. This way she could attract unnecessary resentment to herself from those not favourably disposed to the decisions.

We can see from the account of Sarah and Hagar that even though Hagar was originally Sarah's maid and Sarah wanted her out of the home, Sarah requested her husband to do it rather than be seen as the one who made the decision. God could equally have done it for Sarah but instead, He told Abraham to heed Sarah's voice and act as the leader or head of the family. Abraham then took on the leadership role on behalf of the family, by sending Hagar and Ishmael away. (See Genesis 21:9-14).

Leadership is needed in the family to give direction. God, in His infinite wisdom, has placed the burden of leadership in the family with the husband. Where there is no clear leadership in the family or the leadership is continuously undermined, the result creates confusion in the minds of the children about the direction to follow. Others outside may also have difficulty understanding who to relate with as the leader for the family.

Authority

Authority flows from leadership.

Authority simply means having the legitimate backing to function in your capacity. Where the source of the authority is clearly understood, respect and acceptance are more readily given. On the other hand, friction may arise where the source of the authority is not known or in doubt.

Moses found himself in this dilemma when he was questioned about his leadership authority. The first instance was when he attempted to intervene in the feud between two of his kinsmen.

"Now it came to pass in those days, when Moses was grown, that he went out to his brethren and looked at their burdens. And he saw an Egyptian beating a Hebrew, one of his brethren. So he looked this way and that way, and when he saw no one, he killed the Egyptian and hid him in the sand. And when he went out the second day, behold, two Hebrew men were fighting, and he said to the one who did the wrong, 'Why are you striking your companion?'

"Then he said, 'Who made you a prince and a judge over us? Do you intend to kill me as you killed the Egyptian?'

"So Moses feared and said, 'Surely, this thing is known!'" (Exodus 2:11-14).

Another instance was his encounter with his very close kith and kin, Aaron and Miriam. "Then Miriam and Aaron spoke against Moses because of the Ethiopian woman whom he had married; for he had married an Ethiopian woman. So they said, 'Has the Lord indeed spoken only through Moses? Has He not spoken through us also?' And the Lord heard it (Numbers 12: 1-2). Yet another was with some leaders led by Korah, Dathan and Abiram who challenged his leadership authority" (Numbers 16:1-3).

Apart from the first instance mentioned above, God rose to defend Moses's leadership authority when it was being questioned. This is because God is the source of the authority, and any challenge to the authority vested in Moses was seen by God as a challenge to Him.

Jesus also had His authority questioned by the leaders of the time.

Authority could be derived from the law, delegation, mutual consent, or from the word of God (for those who are spiritually minded).

The first issue is to know and accept the source of the authority. Once the source is accepted, it is expected that the authority flowing or derived from that source should be equally acknowledged and accepted. But if the source is not accepted, it should not be surprising if there is opposition to the authority.

Accepting or yielding to authority means accepting or yielding to the source, while rejecting or opposing the authority is considered as rejecting or opposing the source. This is why the source of the authority being questioned, opposed, or rejected, would normally defend the authority against any force that is opposing or rejecting it.

Leadership carries with it responsibilities as well as authority. Accepting the leadership should normally mean accepting the authority that is vested in the leadership. It is absurd to say you accept a leadership and yet not acknowledge the authority of the leadership.

When relating this to the family and marriage, everyone in the family is entrusted with leadership in one capacity or the other. But when it comes to the overall family, the husband is entrusted with the responsibility of leadership in keeping with God's design.

So in the same way as we accept the leadership within the family, we should also accept the authority flowing from the leadership. Doing otherwise would mean opposing or rejecting the source of that authority—God.

Often times the cause of crisis in a marriage is not refusal to acknowledge the leadership of the spouse, but challenging, denying, or undermining the authority of the spouse.

This can arise, for example, where the spouse directs that the children should not do a particular thing; but shortly after, the other spouse directs otherwise, even though aware of the earlier directive.

Or as the spiritual head and leader of the family, the husband says that in the overall interest of the family he would not want the wife to embark on a particular project. But contrary to this, the wife goes ahead believing and insisting that she is entitled to do as she pleases.

The only clear record of divorce in the Scriptures emanated from a challenge to a husband's authority. King Ahasuerus had made an unusual request to Queen Vashti. No doubt, the request looked stupid, considering that she was the Queen and not just an ordinary woman to be paraded as an object of entertainment before visitors. She must have felt that as a Queen she has a right to her dignity. She called her husband's authority into question when she refused to honour his absurd invitation. The result was a divorce, dethronement, and replacement (See Esther 1: 10-22).

The lesson here for married couples is that of acknowledging and accepting leadership authority.

Remember, all Scriptures were written for our instruction. "All Scripture is given by inspiration of God, and is profitable for doctrine, for reproof, for correction, for instruction in righteousness that the man of God may be complete, thoroughly equipped for every good work" (2 Timothy 3:16-17).

As believers, we should know that each time we despise or undermine the leadership authority of our spouse we are undermining God, Who is the source of such authority. We should realise that the source of leadership authority in a Christian marriage is not necessarily from the secular laws but from God.

Submission

This is another issue that is closely related to leadership and authority.

Submission refers to the act of yielding to another. It could be done willingly or obtained through coercion. However, submission obtained by coercion usually results in resentment, ill-feelings, and ultimately, rebellion. Our focus would be on willing submission, as God in His almightiness does not force or coerce us to submit to Him. He only makes us willing to submit to Him.

Submission is usually to one in authority. However, it could also be to peers or even subordinates.

The opposite of submission is rebellion. So where submission is lacking, rebellion abounds, even where this has not become fully known. God detests rebellion, and we are told in Scriptures that the sin of rebellion is comparable to that of witchcraft. "For rebellion is as the sin of witchcraft, and stubbornness is as iniquity and idolatry" (1 Samuel 15:23).

Issues have often arisen out of marriages because the husband accuses the wife of not being submissive to him. This is the most pervasive term in which submission is seen and viewed in marriages. Of course, it is defendable because it has its root in Scriptures. Men are quick to draw the attention of their wives and others to the relevant aspects of the Scriptures that support this. "Wives, submit to your own husbands, as to the Lord. For the husband is head of the wife, as also Christ is head of the church; and He is the Saviour of the body" (Ephesians 5:22-23).

It is clearly virtuous and profitable for a woman to submit to her husband. Homes where the women are submissive to their husbands are known to experience more peace and harmony than those where the wives are not submissive.

There are other equally important areas where submission is desirable in the home but are generally down-played. The Bible talks about submitting to one another. This aspect is as important as submitting to authority. "Submitting to one another in the fear of God" (Ephesians 5:21).

Submitting to one another means submitting to others who may not be in authority over us, such as our peers and even our subordinates. We do this by acknowledging and submitting to the ideas, counsel, expressions, desires, and feelings of others.

This means that in the home, both the husband and the wife are to acknowledge, respect, and submit to each other's ideas, counsel, expressions, desires and feelings. The husband should never feel that because he is the head he has no need to listen or submit to the wife's opinion. Even the opinions of the children should not just be discountenanced in the family. In the wider society, life would be much better if those in authority learned to listen, respect, and submit to the opinion and the desires of their subjects.

God pointed Abraham in this direction when there was one of the few recorded cases of marriage friction in the Scriptures—the one between Abraham and Sarah.

Sarah wanted Abraham to send Ishmael and his mother away, having become uncomfortable with their presence. Scriptures record that Abraham was very displeased with the suggestion. So we can infer that he would not have succumbed to it. God had to intervene and directed him to listen to his wife's desire.

"And Sarah saw the son of Hagar the Egyptian, whom she had borne to Abraham, scoffing. Therefore she said to Abraham, 'Cast out this bondwoman and her son; for the son of this bondwoman shall not be heir with my son, namely with Isaac.' And the matter was very displeasing in Abraham's sight because of his son.

"But God said to Abraham, 'Do not let it be displeasing in your sight because of the lad or because of your bondwoman. Whatever Sarah has said to you, listen to her voice; for in Isaac your seed shall be called. Yet I will also make a nation of the son of the bondwoman, because he is your seed.'

"So Abraham rose early in the morning, and took bread and a skin of water; and putting it on her shoulder, he gave it and the boy to Hagar, and sent her away. Then she departed and wandered in the Wilderness of Beersheba" (Genesis 21:9-14).

Husbands and wives should learn to listen and submit to each other's ideas, opinions, and feelings. Do not just ignore and dismiss each other because you think your wife or husband is not and cannot be knowledgeable enough to give a meaningful opinion or view on a matter. Acting this way has often left so many marriages in scars.

Conflicts and Resolution

As in most human or social relationships involving the interaction of two or more persons, conflicts abound in marriages also. This is because it is a union of two persons with individually unique peculiarities, now fusing into one. Though the two persons must have more in common, as well as a common bond, for them to be attracted to each other in marriage; the individuality of each often seek ways of expressing itself, unless completely subdued. The uniqueness of each individual reflects in his thought process, perception, ideas, emotions, feelings and opinions.

As social beings, we are naturally entangled in a network of social relationships. For these relationships to be sustained, we have to identify and nurture the things which strengthen them. Similarly, we need to identify those things that tend to weaken, strain, or threaten the relationship and work toward curtailing, eliminating, or managing them.

Conflicts generally have the propensity to damage relationships if not managed well and have ruined many friendships as a result. Nations have gone into wars with each other or had their diplomatic relations strained as a result of conflicts. So also have marriages been broken or left with painful scars as a result of conflicts. But it does not always have to leave such negative imprints behind. If well managed, conflicts could lead to a stronger and healthier relationship, as it could help us to understand the peculiarities of each other better. This, in turn, would help us know how to relate with each other better. Through conflicts, we could know the temperaments of the other, their perceptions and conceptions, and their "likes" and "dislikes", which if managed properly, could lead to a more robust and healthier relationship built on a better understanding of each other.

Generally, conflicts derive from two major sources: 1) misunderstandings and 2) disagreements.

Misunderstandings

These are conflicts arising out of wrong perception or interpretation of the other person's motive, ideas, words, or actions, driven mostly by our individual peculiarities and experiences. When we use our own peculiarities and experiences to judge or interpret a situation or someone else's action without giving due consideration to that person's peculiarities, we may end up misunderstanding the other person. In the same way, when we act based on our own peculiarities and experiences, ignoring the other person's peculiarities and expecting him or her to interpret it the same way as we do, we may end up with a misunderstanding between the other party and us.

Misunderstanding could arise from the simplest of communications, just as it could from the most complex action. What started as a basic misunderstanding can degenerate into a major conflict if not properly handled.

Misunderstanding can be classified into two main categories:

1. Genuine error of interpretation or judgement of the other person's action or utterances

2. Biased interpretation or judgement of the other person's action or utterances as a result of our peculiarities and experiences.

In marriages, a greater number of the conflicts experienced are brought on by misunderstandings.

Often one finds that at the heart of the conflict is unclear, ineffective or misconstrued communication. In this situation, one could see a husband or a wife reacting to an action, inaction or utterance based on a wrong interpretation. Interestingly, it does not always hold true that the wrong interpretation or reaction occurred because the action or utterance being responded to was too complex to understand. Sometimes, what may be considered by one party as a very simple and straight forward statement, action, or inaction can be misinterpreted by the other party and, therefore, lead to a misunderstanding.

It is only when you drill down to the root cause of the conflict that you would realise it was born out of misunderstanding. In situations like this, you would find out that both parties have a common goal or view point but just did not realise this. When all is said and done, what you hear from the contending partners is, "I thought you said this" or "I thought you meant that."

The more complex and dangerous form of misunderstanding is that which arises from bias.

In this instance, the action, inaction, or utterance would have been quite clear to interpret or understand. However, the other party chooses to interpret it from a biased or prejudiced point of view. A noble gesture would be deliberately misconstrued. The other party's actions are viewed with suspicion and believed to be driven by ulterior motives; even a simple and honest compliment is interpreted with bias and reacted to accordingly.

The reality is that most people who respond in this way are victims of their peculiar experiences. Drawing on previous negative incidents, they have come to the point of now generalizing and transferring the result of those encounters into their current relationships.

Misunderstanding can also be fuelled by third party misrepresentations and misinterpretations.

When an action is based on information received from a third party, the possibility of that information having been distorted, misrepresented, or misinterpreted becomes a factor. Actions or reactions based on this type of information can only bring about a conflict of misunderstanding.

Husbands and wives have been known to engage in unnecessary conflicts of misunderstanding because they allowed third parties to mislead them. The third parties may have done it deliberately to achieve that purpose or unintentionally because they truly misinterpreted the information they were reporting on.

The greatest challenge, however, is that if not properly managed and resolved, a "simple misunderstanding" can degenerate into a major and complex conflict.

Disagreements

Conflicts arising from outright disagreements are by far the most catastrophic in relationships.

In this instance, there is a basic or clear understanding of the message or issue at stake. However, either party refuses to accept the other's position, preferring to hold on strongly to their own. There is no common ground and no determination by either the husband or the wife to shift grounds. This could lead to a total disintegration of the marriage relationship if not resolved in good time. This is why we have situations where the couple say they have "irreconcilable differences."

Recall that the scriptures refer to this when it asked a critical question in the book of Amos 3:3. "Can two walk together, unless they are agreed?"

Conflict arising from outright and clear disagreement in a marriage relationship is a recipe for disaster if not dealt with and resolved early. This is even more so if the disagreement touches on the core values that the partners cherish.

An example of a conflict arising out of disagreement is that of David and his wife, Michal. "Then David returned to bless his household. And Michal the daughter of Saul came out to meet David, and said, 'How glorious was the king of Israel today, uncovering himself today in the eyes of the maids of his servants, as one of the base fellows shamelessly uncovers himself!'" (2 Samuel 6:20).

David was an ardent worshipper. He treasured God above any other thing and would not compromise when it came to the issue of worshipping God.

Michal, on the other hand, was not raised the same way and did not have the same zeal and passion for God. As far as she was concerned, David was an extremist who was unnecessarily overzealous for God. Like her father, King Saul, she was more focused on the opinion of people than that of God. Saul repeatedly demonstrated this propensity to pander to people's desire rather than God's and to obtain men's praise rather than God's.

It stands to reason from the address of Michal to David that she must have previously broached this subject of David's "ignominious" behaviour, especially when it came to spiritual matters of God and worship. It is even possible that she had mentioned it a couple of times with David still remaining uncompromising. One can sense the spite in her statement to her husband. So the response from her husband, David, is not surprising.

"So David said to Michal, 'It was before the Lord who chose me instead of your father and all his house, to appoint me ruler over the people of the Lord, over Israel. Therefore I will play music before the Lord. And I will be even more undignified than this, and will be humble in my own sight. But as for the maidservants of whom you have spoken, by them I will be held in honour'" (2 Samuel 6:21-22).

Disagreements in marriages are dysfunctional and could lead couples to start working at different purposes from each other. Unless compromise or shifting of grounds is achieved, such conflicts could become quite fatal to the marriage. Even though unintended at the beginning, failing to agree is an invitation to spiritual separation, starting with the parting of minds. In other words, while still physically and socially married, the reality is that a spiritual separation is already taking place. If allowed to continue, the actual manifestation of a physical and social separation or divorce would only be a matter of time.

Our core values do not have to be asserted in spiritual matters, as that of David and Michal. What is of value to one person may not be to another. So couples need to know what the core values of their spouses are.

For example, a husband who strongly believes in the "headship" of the man over the woman, and a wife who strongly believes in "women's rights, liberation and freedom of women" are an indication of a couple with different core values. Unless there is a clear understanding and genuine determination by each of the partners to compromise, the relationship would be embedded in conflict.

Conflict Resolution

Since conflicts abound in social relationships, including marriage, how do we ensure that they do not wreck havoc on our marital relations?

The first step is to admit that a conflict has arisen in the relationship. As weird and unthinkable as this may seem, it is possible for conflict to exist between two parties in a relationship and yet have both people in denial of any conflict. In this case, they try to convince themselves that all is well, even when all does not seem well.

Having admitted to there being a conflict in the relationship, the next logical thing for the husband or wife to do is to determine to openly talk about it or discuss it with the partner concerned. In doing this, each of the partners should be prepared to do the following:

- Have a willingness to be frank and open minded with the discussions
- See the dialogue as an avenue for resolving the conflict and not for finding faults
- Be ready to accept their individual errors, mistakes, or wrong doing
- Have a willingness to offer genuine apologies for wrong doing
- Be magnanimous to accept apologies without holding back

- Show a commitment to forgive, where necessary, and allow the healing process of any hurt that may have been suffered

However, a critical element of the discussions is ascertaining the cause of the conflict —whether it was a misunderstanding or an outright disagreement. With conflicts of misunderstanding, it is easier in the course of the discussions for the partners to see that their utterances, actions, or intentions have been misunderstood. This can be more easily resolved with a re-assurance of the actual intentions or utterances, followed by an apology. Even where the misunderstanding has been fuelled by deliberate biased interpretation, owing to the peculiarities and experiences of one of the partners, the resolution could still be easier.

In situations of outright disagreements, finding a resolution can be more tasking. This is due to the fact that in this situation both partners have a clear understanding of the issues at stake and the views or position of each partner. They are, however, not only diametrically opposed to each other's views or position but equally unwilling to yield on theirs. Here, each one is saying, "I hear you loud and clear but I do not agree with you neither would I go along with you."

The ways to work out a resolution would then be:

- Get a compromise from both partners, that is, find a mid-way approach
- Have one partner submit to the other

Whichever approach is used, care must be taken to ensure that it is done without bitterness or a feeling of defeat. There are situations were a compromise or submission extracted today would only leave a festering wound that would develop into a bigger conflict in time. Where a partner has had to submit but with a feeling of having been subdued or conquered, a resolution of the conflict may be temporary as the situation is likely to boil over in the distant future. To achieve true resolution of the conflict, both parties must see their actions as a genuine sacrifice freely given in love for the good of their marriage relationship.

However, there is a means that is by far the most effective way of resolving such marriage conflicts of disagreement without leaving any taste of bitterness. This is through an arbiter in whom both partners have absolute confidence in his counsel. Being a common denominator (in terms of trust and conviction in the quality and integrity of counsel), both partners would readily yield to him. They would believe that the actions they took following the counsel of the arbiter are the most appropriate ones. This is all because both partners have absolute confidence in the same arbiter.

If, on the other hand, one of the partners does not have confidence in the arbiter, he would either reject the counsel or accept it grudgingly. Therefore, there is the need for an arbiter who commands mutual trust and confidence from both partners.

For Christians who are married, it is expected that the arbiter would be God, speaking through His Word in Scriptures and backed by the witnessing of the Holy Spirit.

Whenever a Bible-believing and God-fearing couple find themselves in a situation of conflict (especially that of outright disagreement), they must be ready to submit themselves to the Word of God. This is the surest way for obtaining the right counsel out of the situation. Since they fear God and believe in His Word, they would usually yield to it with conviction in their hearts that there is no better solution than what they have found in the Word. Hence there would be no bitter taste left behind unless their belief is questionable.

Let us take a look at the issue between Abraham and Sarah again.

This certainly was a case of outright conflict of disagreement between the two. Abraham heard Sarah's suggestion loud and clear. He was not mistaken about what Sarah meant or her purpose for such a suggestion. He was, however, greatly opposed to it as he could not come to terms with the thought of having to send away his own son. The idea could have been repulsive to him. It was not in his character to shirk his responsibilities, and he was not going to allow himself to be led into doing so now. The issue at the centre of the disagreement was not that of sending Hagar away but that of banishing his son. Recall that earlier on when Sarah complained about Hagar to him, he gave Sarah the approval to do with Hagar as she pleased. The aftermath of this approval was that Hagar had to flee the home following Sarah's retaliatory treatment to her. Even though Hagar was gone from the home on account of this, we were never told that Abraham was sore because of her departure nor confronted Sarah on the issue. So it can be seen that the sore point of the disagreement is the issue of having to banish his son, Ishmael.

"Then Sarai said to Abram, 'My wrong be upon you! I gave my maid into your embrace; and when she saw that she had conceived, I became despised in her eyes. The Lord judge between you and me.' So Abram said to Sarai, 'Indeed your maid is in your hand; do to her as you please.' And when Sarai dealt harshly with her, she fled from her presence" (Genesis 16:5-6).

Now look at the other account.

"And Sarah saw the son of Hagar the Egyptian, whom she had borne to Abraham, scoffing. Therefore she said to Abraham, 'Cast out this bondwoman and her son; for the son of this bondwoman shall not be heir with my son, namely with Isaac.' And the matter was very displeasing in Abraham's sight because of his son. But God said to Abraham, 'Do not let it be displeasing in your sight because of the lad or because of your bondwoman. Whatever Sarah has said to you, listen to her voice; for in Isaac your seed shall be called. Yet I will also make a nation of the son of the bondwoman, because he is your seed.'

"So Abraham rose early in the morning, and took bread and a skin of water; and putting it on her shoulder, he gave it and the boy to Hagar, and sent her away. Then she departed and wandered in the Wilderness of Beersheba" (Genesis 21:9-14).

As for Sarah, having patiently tried to accommodate Hagar and the son, Ishmael, before then, the only viable option open to her to protect her home and marriage was the banishment of Hagar and Ishmael. Nothing short of that would do.

Obviously, Abraham and Sarah would never have come to terms on this issue without bitterness or hurt to one of them. The good news, however, is that they both had deep respect, trust, and faith in God and His Word. The moment God intervened and spoke His Word of counsel to Abraham to listen to his wife, Sarah, the issue was put to rest with no bitterness on either side thereafter. From this account, we can see that for a Christian marriage, the only influence that can bring a lasting, peaceful resolution of conflicts of disagreements is God, speaking through His Word or Holy Spirit.

As with the case of Abraham, God does not have to speak to us in the heat of the arguments. He could speak to us when we are sober enough to hear Him, by reminding us of His Word that we already know but currently are ignoring. He could also speak through the ministration of the Holy Spirit. By the time we come to realisation, that thing we thought was impossible to yield to would become like nothing; and both partners would be back in one spirit, united in love.

Note that this holds true when both husband and wife share the same beliefs, that is, when they believe in and fear the same God.

If either the husband or the wife is an unbeliever, he or she may not have that same level of trust or confidence in God. In such a situation, they are not operating at the same level or reading from the same page, neither do they have a common denominator. This may lead to the unbelieving partner jettisoning the counsel from the Word of God and maintaining the original uncompromising position or views. Even where such a partner yields to the counsel from the Word, he or she may do so grudgingly and feel coerced.

This is why the Scriptures advised believers not to be unequally yoked with unbelievers. "Do not be unequally yoked together with unbelievers. For what fellowship has righteousness with lawlessness? And what communion has light with darkness?" (2 Corinthians 6:14).

The problem sometimes is that consciously or unconsciously we have entangled ourselves in marriages with those who do not share our spiritual beliefs. When conflicts arise, we expect the other partner to yield to the Word of God that he or she has never truly believed in. Certainly, that is delusion! How can a partner who has always admitted to being a "free thinker" suddenly surrender or yield to the counsel in the Scriptures without resorting to finding his answers from his own source? The same goes for those Christians who are in marriage relationships with those who profess other faiths.

Owing to the importance of this topic under discussion to the survival and stability of marriage relationships, I would want us to look at another scenario before preceding further—the situation between Joseph and Mary.

"Now the birth of Jesus Christ was as follows: After His mother Mary was betrothed to Joseph, before they came together, she was found with child of the Holy Spirit. Then Joseph her husband, being a just man, and not wanting to make her a public example, was minded to put her away secretly. But while he thought about these things, behold, an angel of the Lord appeared to him in a dream, saying, 'Joseph, son of David, do not be afraid to take to you Mary your wife, for that which is conceived in her is of the Holy Spirit. And she will bring forth a Son, and you shall call His name JESUS, for He will save His people from their sins.'

"So all this was done that it might be fulfilled which was spoken by the Lord through the prophet, saying, 'Behold, the virgin shall be with child, and bear a Son, and they shall call His name Immanuel,' which is translated, 'God with us. Then Joseph, being aroused from sleep, did as the angel of the Lord commanded him and took to him his wife" (Mathew 1:18-24).

Mary was betrothed (engaged) to Joseph. Since they were both believers in the Lord, and in line with their custom, they have refrained from having any sexual relations until marriage. Suddenly, Joseph found out that his fiancée was pregnant. She told him the baby she was carrying was a miraculous conception by the Holy Spirit and maintained her fidelity to Joseph.

Since such a thing had never happened before in the history of mankind, it must have been difficult for Joseph to believe. This is even more so, since he was not privy to the same revelation through any spiritual source before the manifestation of the pregnancy. Ordinarily, going by the custom, the engagement should not only have been called off, but she should have been publicly disgraced as well. However, because of the deep love that Joseph had for her, he was thinking of devising a way of secretly calling off the engagement without exposing her to the public ordeal that her action called for.

Imagine how difficult it would have been to reconcile this conflict. Joseph, on the one hand, is alleging infidelity and betrayal, with pregnancy as proof. Meanwhile, Mary, on the other hand, is maintaining innocence and faithfulness, repeatedly explaining that the pregnancy is an act of divine visitation. Even in today's world, I am sure it would take great faith to believe Mary's explanation.

But because Joseph was a man with deep respect and fear for God, as soon as God spoke to him through an angel in his sleep, he yielded wholeheartedly. What he thought was difficult to reconcile with became resolved immediately with no bitterness or pain following. His marriage was restored and their purpose and destiny in marriage was fulfilled.

With man, certain issues may seem contradictory and unworkable, leading to the conclusion that there are irreconcilable differences or disagreements in the marriage relationship. But with God, nothing is impossible to reconcile—but only if you trust and let Him be your arbiter.

The problem we are having today is that we are reluctant in going to the "manufacturer" of marriage for help when things go wrong. Instead, we are approaching other sources or trying out quick-fix manuals put together by those who themselves do not fully understand the complexity of the product. We are looking for solutions where they do not truly exist.

The Marriage Foundation

Separation and Divorce

Separation

Separation means being detached or dissociated from a thing, person, or relationship. For the purpose of this book, our focus would be on people and relationships, especially marriage relationships.

Separation denotes a lack of oneness or unity of thought, purpose, spirit, or deeds. It can be emotional, spiritual, physical, and informal as well as formal/legal. Interestingly, whenever the issue of separation is raised, what readily comes to mind is physical and formal/legal split. This is so because they are the points at which separation becomes evidently manifest. However, it should be noted that the other forms of separation are as disastrous, if not more catastrophic, than the physical and formal/legal ones.

Let us take a look at some of these:

Emotional Separation

This can also take the form of psychological separation. In this situation, the parties concerned could still be physically living together, but either one or both have no feelings for the other. Whether one or both are hurting, it is usually not felt by the other. There is a general insensitivity of one party or both to the emotional needs of the other. This could initially start with some aspects of their relationship but gradually spread to others. At the height of it, you find that what gives pleasure to and feeds the emotion of one is completely different from what does same to the other. For example, there are some couples who are living together but are emotionally detached from each other in terms of love-making. Either one or both have come to be deriving their pleasure from outside of their marriage, without the least care for the feelings of the other.

This is just one basic example out of many others. You find cases in which couples are living in emotional and psychological trauma from the other partner. Though living together, they are emotionally and psychologically separated.

Abraham and Sarah would have found themselves in this situation but for the intervention of God. The issue of Ishmael and his mother, Hagar, was beginning to cause emotional separation between Abraham and Sarah. But thanks be to God for His timely divine intervention!

Spiritual Separation

This type of separation occurs where there is a fundamental difference in beliefs, orientation and spiritual allegiance. Our beliefs generally dictate the course of our thoughts, views and actions. So where these thoughts, views, and actions are predicated on beliefs and spiritual allegiances that are different, the outcomes are bound to be divergent. This ultimately leads to spiritual separation.

Spiritual matters are very deep. Hence, without a common ground, differences occasioned by them could cause deep separation. It is for this reason that the Scripture advices that we should not be yoked unequally with those who share different beliefs. "Do not be unequally yoked together with unbelievers. For what fellowship has righteousness with lawlessness? And what communion has light with darkness?" (2 Corinthians 6:14).

Note that the above Scripture is not restricted to relationships between Christians and non-Christians alone. Even among so-called Christians, we need to be watchful when entering into marriage relationships with those whose beliefs are diametrically opposed to ours. Otherwise, there would be a spiritual separation in the relationship along the way.

For example, in the marriage relationship between David and Michal, we see a couple who were spiritually separated. While David believed that God was deserving of all the honour and therefore considered it as nothing to sacrifice his own honour as a King before God, Michal thought otherwise. Michal believed, like her father, Saul, that the honour of being King must not be sacrificed on the altar of worship of the Almighty God. These are two extreme positions from the perspective of opposing beliefs from two people of the same faith.

Recall that David manifested this same disposition when in response to his craving, some of his followers risked their lives to get him water. He considered that sacrifice as befitting of God only, and instead of drinking the water, poured it out as an offering to God. (See 2 Samuel 23: 15 – 17).

If we marry partners who do not see and believe in God the way we do, or who do not share in our zeal for God, we might just be preparing the ground for spiritual separation along the way.

Physical Separation

This is the aspect of separation that is of common knowledge because of its obvious nature. At this point, the husband and wife are no longer living together, either through mutual agreement, dissension or force of law.

Not all physical separations are conflict related. There are abounding cases where this is dictated by economic, political, and social considerations. In our society of today, there are quite a number of husbands and wives who are physically separated due to exigencies of work or business. Such separations have always been known to occur, as was the case with Moses and David. Moses had to leave his wife with his Father-in-law, Jethro, to go to Egypt out of obedience to God's instruction to lead His people out of Egypt. After accomplishing the mission, he reunited with his wife.

David also had to leave his wife, Michal, when fleeing for his life from King Saul. But upon settling on the throne, he demanded to have his wife reunited back with him.

Our focus is on physical separation occasioned by conflict. These are the types that occur because either one or both parties have decided that they are no longer compatible to live together at that point in time. Even though they may still be considered married, they no longer share a common bond in terms of living together. There is a curtailment of the privileges and the obligations they now have to each other as husband and wife. In most cases, it is a prelude to the final state of divorce. In a few instances, however, it has been used as a period of sorting out the differences between the husband and wife, leading to reconciliation and eventual reunion. Sometimes, for some, it takes getting this far for them to realise how much their marriage relationship has fallen apart. It may well be the "wake-up call" they need to appreciate what they had and realise that they are at the verge of losing it unless they act decisively. But for most, it is a point of no return.

Usually, before it gets to the state of physical separation, the couple would have experienced those other forms of drifting apart, that is, emotional or spiritual or both. The only unfortunate thing is that one or both parties may have chosen to ignore those early signs. A major way of avoiding physical separation is by dealing with the early forms as soon as the signs are noticed.

Finally, separation can be informal or formal/legal depending on the understanding between the couple and the circumstances surrounding the separation.

However, God's plan for marriage is that the husband and wife should not be separated but be united in Him as one. They are expected to be united in spirit, in thought, in words, in purpose, and in deeds. This can only happen if they are united in spirit through God. In such a situation, even if they are physically separated owing to certain exigencies, they would still be as one. This is because, though not physically present with each other, they remain united in spirit, thought, words, purpose, and deed.

God expressly said it is not good for man to be alone, but he should have a partner that compares to him. In order words, man needs to be united to a partner who compares to him in spirit, thought, words, purpose, and deeds. In the same vein, this applies to the woman also.

If God, in His infinite wisdom and knowledge, has declared that it is not good for the man or the woman to be alone, why do we think we know better? It is a known and common truth that where two are working together in unity, they can achieve much more than having to work separately.

Separation is a seed of disunity which must be seen and dealt with appropriately for what it is. Married couples must do all they can to ensure that it does not take root in their relationships.

Divorce

Divorce is the termination or dissolution of marriage other than through death. It is the ultimate declaration by the parties in a marriage that it is over.

Usually, divorce is predicated on the premise that irreconcilable differences exist between the partners—the husband and the wife. At that point, either one or both partners conceive that it is in their best interest to end the marriage relationship. They believe it is no longer workable. But who says the difference is irreconcilable and the marriage no longer workable? Is it man or God? And whose report should you believe—that of man or God? The answer to this, I believe, is well expressed in the Scriptures in the Book of Lamentation. "Who is he who speaks and it comes to pass, when the Lord has not commanded it?" (Lamentation 3:37).

God's plan for marriage is that the husband and wife stay together until death separates them. This is because He is the bond by which they are joined together. The strength of a bond is a factor whenever attempting to separate any substance held together by that bond.

God has equally warned that no man, either by themselves or through institutions established by man, should separate the husband and wife that He has joined together. This means that the husband, wife, family, or man-made institutions, such as courts have no spiritual right to dissolve a marriage without being answerable to God.

Even when it became permissible following the time of Moses, God had to remind us through Jesus that it was never, and is still not His original plan for marriage.

"Now it came to pass, when Jesus had finished these sayings that He departed from

Galilee and came to the region of Judea beyond the Jordan. And great multitudes followed Him, and He healed them there. The Pharisees also came to Him, testing Him, and saying to Him, 'Is it lawful for a man to divorce his wife for just any reason?'

"And He answered and said to them, 'Have you not read that He who made them at the beginning 'made them male and female,' and said, 'For this reason a man shall leave his father and mother and be joined to his wife, and the two shall become one flesh' So then, they are no longer two but one flesh. Therefore, what God has joined together, let not man separate.'

"They said to Him, 'Why then did Moses command to give a certificate of divorce, and to put her away?'

He said to them, 'Moses, because of the hardness of your hearts, permitted you to divorce your wives, but from the beginning it was not so. And I say to you, whoever divorces his wife, except for sexual immorality, and marries another, commits adultery; and whoever marries her who is divorced commits adultery'" (Mathew 19:1-9).

From the foregoing, we can see that divorce was only in the permissive will of God and not in His perfect will for man in marriage. It is always better to operate under the perfect will of God than in His permissive will. There are consequences for operating under the permissive will of God. As such, anyone hiding under the permissive will of God to divorce should be ready to account for his or her actions before God.

Let us examine two situations where the children of Israel operated under the permissive will of God.

The first occurred when they complained about being fed continuously with manna instead of the meat they were used to. God told Moses that He would grant their request and He gave them quails as meat. They were happy. But the consequence of that was the death of so many because of the plague that came with it. (See Numbers 11: 1-34).

The second example of the Israelites operating under God's permissive will came when the Israelites demanded an earthly king like other nations—even though God had told them that they would be different from the other nations and He would be their King. God told Samuel not to worry but rather should accede to their request. The consequences of that, however, was that they would now be subservient to their kings who would lord themselves over the people. (See I Samuel 8: 4-22).

Divorce is man-made. It was not in God's original plan for marriage and is still not, as reaffirmed by Jesus. Therefore, any counsel in favour of divorce can never be from the Spirit of God. The problem is that we often seek for solutions where they cannot be found.

No Man of God, filled with and led by the Spirit of God, would advocate and encourage divorce! Jesus demonstrated this by His action in the encounter with the woman accused of adultery (See John 8: 2-11). Even though she was caught in the act and confronted by witnesses who testified against her, Jesus pardoned her and gave her a second chance. He demonstrated the need for forgiveness, one to the other, even in such situations. He made us to see through his response to the accusers of the adulterous woman that even the partners who have been cheated against cannot claim not to be guilty of one sin or the other. But God in His infinite mercy is willing to forgive us if we go to Him in true repentance and ask for pardon.

God says it loudly and clearly in His Word. "For the Lord God of Israel says that He hates divorce" (Malachi 2:16).

The reasons for divorce could be numerous and diverse. But one thing stands sure—that the genuine fear of God conquers all those numerous and diverse reasons for divorce.

Going by the current day reasoning of man, Adam had all the plausible reasons to divorce Eve. He could have recounted:

- How Eve's action brought him down from his position of glory

- How he lost everything in the Garden of Eden
- How he is now having to go through travails because of Eve
- How he has been sentenced and made a victim of death because of Eve

But because he feared God, he never contemplated the option of divorce.

Also, God, in His anger and disappointment over what Adam and Eve did, could have used it as a reason to dissolve their marriage. But because He is faithful to His word that says He hates divorce, He never dissolved their marriage. Instead, He reinforced it by bringing order into their marriage. This clearly shows that divorce was not in God's original plan for marriage.

Love is an essential ingredient of marriage. Love, the scripture says, covers all sins. "Love suffers long and is kind; love does not envy; love does not parade itself, is not puffed up; does not behave rudely, does not seek its own, is not provoked, thinks no evil; does not rejoice in iniquity, but rejoices in the truth; bears all things, believes all things, hopes all things, endures all things. Love never fails" (I Corinthians 13:4-8).

This type of love is, however, not possible with man, except one who loves and fears God. Hence, show me a man or woman that fears the Lord, and I will show you a man or woman who is capable of loving to the point of allowing all sins and wrongs against him or her to be covered by that love.

Before you approach that man or institution for intervention in your marriage, you should pause and ask yourself:

- Do I really want to lose my partner or gain back the loving partner that I married?
- Do I really want a divorce or I would prefer to have my marriage restored with the love and joy I use to have with my partner at the onset of our marriage?
- What record does the person or institution I contemplate approaching for intervention in my marriage have in terms of helping to build up or destroy marriages?

If we do not see divorce as an option, we would not look to it as an option.

Knowing God's position on divorce, we are to show love, compassion, and support to those who have found themselves in that situation, just as Jesus did for the Samaritan woman by the well. (See John 4: 5-26).We are not to condemn and judge them. Instead, we are to show them the love of Christ and let them know that Jesus loves them and died for them, in spite of themselves.

Key Points

Separation and divorce are not part of God's original plan for marriage. They are man-made. While our marital status is not a qualifier for making heaven, what we do with our marriage can have consequences for our faith.

If we do not see divorce as an option, we would not look to it as an option. We can avoid all the hurts, resentment and scars that divorce brings with it and have a healthy, peaceful, joyful, and lovely marriage if we relate in our marriages with the love and fear of God. Let us refrain from seeking solutions to our marriage problems where the solutions cannot truly be found.

Finally, we should remember to show love, compassion, and support to those who have already fallen victim to divorce. God loves them equally the way He loves us.

The Fear Factor

Fear either compels someone to do something or restrains the person from doing something, more so when driven by reverential fear. Fear is not just that type which is occasioned by fright, dread, or terror. Here, we are also referring to the fear of not wanting to hurt or fall out of favour with someone much cherished or revered, as the case with God. In the bid to please God, the one who truly fears Him would do all within his or her ability to ensure that God is not offended with him or her. Such a person would always be mindful of his or her relationship with God and would price that relationship highly and strive always not to lose it. It is in this regard that the fear of God becomes the necessary factor in keeping and sustaining a marriage.

There needs to be a constant realisation that God is a present factor in every marriage ordained by Him and that He has expectations from the partners in the marriage. Where this realisation is present, couples who fear God would be mindful of how they relate with one another. They would be guided by this fear of God to do the things that would please not just themselves but God as well. They would consciously follow the road map that God has provided for married couples. Whenever they derail, such couples would be remorseful and retrace their steps so as not to severe their much-cherished relationship with God.

A married man or woman who truly loves and fears God would be restrained from engaging in extra-marital affairs, not just for the sake of the partner who may never know but because of not wanting to offend God. Even where one partner is unfaithful with no fear of God, the other partner, if he or she has the fear of God, would still be compelled to remain faithful.

Similarly, a married man or woman who truly loves and fears God would not be abusive to the spouse, knowing how special the spouse is in the sight of God. Such a person would allow God, acting through His Word and the Holy Spirit to be his or her guide and counsellor. Even where personal feelings or emotions run contrary, because of the fear of God, he or she would be restrained from yielding to those feelings or emotions.

Hence, it would be easier to forgive offences by the spouse, knowing that God would not be pleased with anything contrary. The love and fear of God would constrain a spouse to love the other irrespective of the situation and to resolve issues and differences, lovingly, without allowing it to linger. It would restrain a spouse from harbouring bitterness against the other for wrongdoings. Where there is the fear of God in a marriage, each partner is conscious of his or her accountability to God for actions or inactions against the other partner. Often, at the heart of that lingering and persistent crisis in a marriage, is the absence or lack of the fear of God. In such situations, one or both partners believe that they are free to act toward the other the way they like.

While our natural emotions and love toward our spouses may fail, owing to circumstances and situations, the love of God never fails. Only by yielding to God and allowing His love flow in and through us can we transfer that same love to our partners.

This is why I say, show me a man or woman who loves and fears God, and I will show you a man or woman who is capable of loving the partner.

When everything else fails, the fear of God is the only thing that can uphold and sustain a marriage. Death is one natural phenomenon that dissolves a marriage permanently. After death, there is no more marriage, not even in heaven. Yet, the fear of God can keep death away while sustaining a marriage.

If Haman had the fear of God, his life and marriage would have been sustained. He would have listened and acted on the counsel of his wise men and his wife, Zeresh (See Esther 6: 13),

Similarly, Nabal would not have died the way he did, and his marriage to Abigail would have been sustained. But he lacked the fear of God and had no regard for God's anointed— David (See 1Samuel 25: 2-38).

Any man or woman is capable of anything; even where the original intentions are good and noble. The only thing that can truly keep someone in check is the fear of God. It would make us listen to our spouse and reconcile that seemingly irreconcilable difference, as was the case with Abraham and Sarah over Ishmael. The fear of God would make a man or a woman submit to the spouse and do things that, ordinarily, he or she would have considered impossible.

One of the frustrations in marriage counselling is providing godly counsel to someone who lacks the fear of God. A marriage where there is no fear of God is a disaster waiting to happen. This is why God would not lead a true believer to marry someone who has no fear of God.

Unscriptural Terms to Avoid in Marriage

There are some words that have crept into use in our marriages without any Scriptural backing. Worse still, they are of no positive value to marriages. The use of such words or terms only helps to infuse undesirable elements into our marriage, with capacity for weakening or destroying it. The danger is that often times we use these terms without being conscious of their implications to our marriage. Here are a few examples.

Bread winner

Whenever the word *winner* is used, it presupposes that there is also a "loser."

God has set up the marriage relationship so that the husband and the wife are comparable to each other and complement each other. They are not in a competition for power or in a personality contest. They are, therefore, both winners. So, irrespective of who brings in more of the economic or financial resources, there is no winner and no loser. The word *bread winner* has the negative connotation that makes it seem like the other partner is a lesser contributor to the marriage and that his or her efforts are hardly appreciated. As a rule, this term should not even be used in the home at all, as it has the capacity of creating rivalry not only between husband and wife but between and among siblings as well. Rivalry is unhealthy in a marriage, home, or family.

There may be situations where it seems obvious that the husband or the wife is contributing more in terms of financial or economic resources. However, there would always be some non-financial contributions that are being made by the other partner which are not easily quantifiable. Hence, the need to refrain from ever using the term *bread winner* in a marriage relationship, the home or family. Besides creating unhealthy and unnecessary rivalry, using this term has the potential of making those who feel that their contributions are considered less important, to hold back, stop, or reduce their level of contribution.

Housewife

This term is the creation of man with a derogatory intent. In the original context of marriage, as in the reckoning of God, a wife is a wife. The attempt at classifying a wife by her occupation or vocation is to say the least, malicious. It is even most unfortunate that this tag is only applied to wives who are considered not to be engaged in an occupation, trade, or vocation. The focus and emphasis is on their state of current engagement and gives no recognition to their acquired training or skills.

Is it not curious that while the term housewife is freely used, we hardly hear of "officewife," "businesswife" and other such terms? This clearly shows the intent and purpose of the use of the term *housewife*. It is meant to denigrate wives who have chosen to give full time attention to the management of their homes. So whether she is a qualified lawyer or accountant by training, the fact that she has decided to devote her time fully to the management of the home makes her regarded as a housewife, as opposed to her counterpart who chooses to practice her profession.

All through the Scriptures, there is nowhere wives were referred to as housewives. In the account of the virtuous wife in Proverbs 31:10–31, she was described as one who was occupied with the management of her home. The term housewife, as used in its derogatory form, has caused displacements in a number of homes, with wives opting for career jobs and businesses, even at the expense of the proper welfare of their homes.

Just as it happened in the Garden of Eden with the serpent asking the woman if God indeed said they should not eat of every tree of the Garden, I can see the same disastrous trick here again. I can see wives being asked cunningly; *Did God indeed say you should be housewives? Do you not know that you would become equal to men once you stop being housewives?*

While there is nothing wrong with a wife taking up a career, we must be careful not to denigrate those who have chosen to give full-time attention to the management of their homes. The contributions from such wives are unquantifiable and could even surpass those of their working counterparts. Therefore, avoid the use of any and every tag that has derogatory tendencies toward wives or women.

The Marriage Foundation

– By McPeters Atsagbede –

An environmentally friendly book printed and bound in
England by www.printondemand-worldwide.com

This book is made entirely of chain-of-custody materials

The Marriage Foundation

www.fast-print.net/store.php

THE MARRIAGE FOUNDATION
Copyright © McPeters Atsagbede 2014
E-mail: matsagbede@gmail.com

A catalogue record for this book is available from the British Library

All Scriptures, unless otherwise stated, are taken from The New King James Version of the Bible, Copyright 1990, Thomas Nelson Inc.

ISBN 978-178456-031-7

First published 2014 by
FASTPRINT PUBLISHING
Peterborough, England.

This book is dedicated to all marriages that are built on the foundation of Christ and those that would be built or rebuilt on the foundation of Christ; especially through the reading of this book.

Table of Contents

The Marriage Foundation

Acknowledgements

I am eternally grateful to God for giving me the inspiration to write this book and for His grace that has seen this work through.

For devoting time to meticulously proofread and edit the manuscript, my special appreciation goes to Jeanne Marie Leach. Your comments about the book have been a source of encouragement.

I cannot fully express my sincere appreciation to Pastor Dupe (Dupsy) and Pastor (Mrs) Jackie Omotosho for the invaluable roles they have played in my spiritual life. God used both of you to guide me in the way of my Spiritual Calling and stir up my gifting in Ministry. You have always been a source of support and inspiration. Pastor Dupsy, thank you, once again, for writing the "Foreword" to this book.

To Pastor John and Pastor (Mrs) Stella Toritsemotse I also say a special thank you for all your prayers, support and encouragement. You have aided my spiritual growth tremendously by continually providing me with opportunities to develop in knowledge. Your sincere love and warmth towards the brethren would always be remembered.

To all the Pastors and those from whom I have received spiritual nourishment over the years, I express my gratitude. May you all be constantly refreshed by the Holy Spirit, in Jesus' Name.

I also acknowledge my spiritual family, The Redeemed Christian Church of God, Fountain of Love, Naas; as well as The Redeemed Christian Church of God, Open Heavens, Glasnevin. Your prayers, love and support are much appreciated.

Finally, my profound appreciation goes to my wife, Sandra and our children, Daisy, Dennie and Deborah. I thank you especially for your love, understanding and support all through the years. In you I have found a mirror to constantly reflect, evaluate and bring myself under God's divine pruning, so as to be the husband and father that God expects me to be.

Foreword

I enjoyed the privilege of being pastor to McPeters and his lovely wife Sandra for some years. The love, joy and peace in their marriage and their home were evident to all. These and their wonderful hospitality made their home the most successful house fellowship in the church. The success of their marriage qualifies McPeters to write this book.

Uncle McPee, as we fondly call him, is a man of great wisdom and revelation! His explanation on roles and responsibilities in marriage is so revealing. He offers biblical answers and guidance to the usual questions on marriage in our society. He also gives a good argument on why we need to do away with the terms "Breadwinner" and "Housewife".

The book - The Marriage Foundation - takes us back to the one who created marriage, to establish a biblical foundation for marriage.

This book is a compelling read for wisdom, revelation and counsel for those about to marry and those who are already married. It invites us to make God an integral part of our marriage. It also helps us to understand the purpose, roles and responsibilities inherent in marriage, while encouraging us to live up to God's expectation of us in the marriage.

Pastor Dupe Omotosho
RCCG Jesus City Church
1218 Copeland Oaks Drive
Morrisville NC 27560

Introduction

The Family is considered the basic unit of society. But much more than being the basic unit, it is the bedrock of society. Therefore, it is not presumptuous to say that there can be no meaningful discussion about family and society without some mention of marriage.

Marriage is a subject that has always generated a lot of interest in society—both to those who believe in it and those who claim not to believe in it. This is understandable, considering the role marriage plays in the family and society.

In this book I have chosen to look at marriage critically from its very root or foundation. Where the foundation of a building is faulty, there is every tendency that whatever structure is put on that foundation will collapse. So, also, it is with marriage. This is why the Scripture says in Psalm 11:3 that "If the foundations are destroyed what can the righteous do?" The only viable and reasonable thing to do is to return to that foundation and seek to rebuild or correct it.

While quite a list of literature, seminars, and counselling abound on this subject, few are focused on the foundational truth about marriage. It is made worse in today's world where we try to be socially and politically correct in what we say. Attempts also are being made to subject the Word of God to this social and political correctness. The truth, however, is that God's Word is forever sure and bears the same truth whether in Africa, America, Asia, or Europe. It is also as true today as it was yesterday. So any "truth" that changes with time, persons, environment, and culture cannot be God's truth and should be subject to proper scrutiny.

A lot of attention and time is being focused and spent on the things that "spice up" a marriage instead of on the things that are the solid foundation on which every marriage must rest. Some of these marriage "spices" have socio-cultural and ethnic relativity while the things that are foundational hold true universally. Sometimes, those spices have only become needed because we want to make up for certain deficiencies in our "marriage cooking." Just like in normal cooking, the spices may not have been necessary if the "marriage cooking" was right in the first place.

Marriage was never meant to be burdensome and should never be viewed as such. Instead, God meant it to be a burden lifter. The fact that some people now think and see marriage as a burden is not new. After Jesus explained God's original plan for marriage in Matthew 19:1-10, it is recorded that His disciples said: "If such is the case of the man with his wife, it is better not to marry." Apostle Paul also took this line of thought when he said, "For I wish that all men were even as I myself" (1 Corinthians 7: 7). He then went ahead to advise those not yet married to remain unmarried just like him. This shows that some of the Apostles also viewed marriage as burdensome.

If God had said in His Word that it is not good for a man to be alone but should have a wife for a companion, and man now says otherwise, whose report should we believe? Certainly that of God! Jesus is our sure foundation. There is no other foundation that can be laid by anyone except that which had been laid by Jesus (1 Corinthians 3: 11). No other foundation can sustain marriage except the Word of God. Those disciples declared being unmarried as better than being married. This is because they were looking at marriage principally from two angles: something to satisfy sexual desires (and possibly raise offspring), and something that should be easily dissolved at will. They were, therefore, uncomfortable with Jesus' exposition. But the purpose of marriage goes far beyond that.

Being married or unmarried is not necessarily the criteria for being a good Christian or making it to heaven. But what you do with your marriage can have consequences that could affect you before God. For example:

- Did you become a liar in the course of your marriage by lying to your spouse?
- Did you become abusive in your relationship with your spouse?
- Did you become unfaithful and unreliable due to your infidelity to your spouse?
- Did you become a wicked person through acting wickedly to your spouse?
- Did you act to support and encourage or to pull and discourage your spouse away from God?
- Did you act responsibly in raising the children that God entrusted to you through marriage?

Remember that we are all accountable to a God who knows and sees all things. Some typical examples of how our actions in marriage can affect us before God are: Onan and Tamar (Genesis 38: 6-10) and David and Michal (2 Samuel 6: 16-23).

Until Onan married Tamar, following the tradition of his people, he was safe. But once married to Tamar, he became answerable to God for his actions towards his wife, Tamar. Hence he was struck dead for dealing with Tamar treacherously by deliberately emitting on the ground each time during love making.

In Michal's case, for despising and dishonouring David, her husband, God closed her womb and caused her to be barren until death.

It is in this light that we need to carefully understand what God expects of us in marriage and how we can indeed enjoy and have a glorious marriage that meets the expectation of God.